Navigating Diversity

An Advocate's Guide
Through the Maze of
Race, Gender, Religion and More

Patty Bates-Ballard
& Gregory Smith

Navigating Diversity
Copyright © 2008
Patty Bates-Ballard and Gregory Smith

All rights reserved

ISBN: **1-4392-0858-1**

Second printing 2009

Printed in the USA

Disclaimer: Reliance upon and utilization of
any information in this book shall be at your
sole risk. The authors assume no responsibility
for, and are not liable for any damages of any
kind resulting from the use of, or reliance on,
the information contained in this book.

For Natjar, Adam, Stanton,
Stayton, Kory, Kaden
and all of their contemporaries

May their conversations
be satisfying and enriching.

Table of Contents

Issues

1. Age discrimination
2. Affirmative Action
3. American Indians today
4. Arabs and airplanes
5. Asian Americans born in the US
6. "Blacks are good at sports and music"
7. "Blacks will prevail over White people"
8. "Boy"
9. Chambers of Commerce (Black, White)
10. Chip on the shoulder
11. Color-blindness
12. Crime and ethnicity
13. Education - different success rates
14. "Elite silver-spooner"
15. "Go back where you came from"
16. "God d@#! America"
17. "Hard-working White Americans"
18. Holocaust denial
19. Homosexuality wrong according to the Bible
20. Hyphenated Americans
21. "Illegal aliens" / "United States of Mexico"
22. Insensitive joke
23. "Iron my shirt"
24. Jewish people and money
25. "Liberal atheists"
26. Majority rule
27. Melting pot
28. Muslim women subservient

Table of Contents, cont.

Acknowledgements

This book is a collaborative effort that reflects the input of thousands of people. We began writing this book in 2004, but the information we cover goes back to the early 1990's when we entered the world of diversity training.

Patty originally developed ACE-ing Conflict while working and collaborating with Liz Flores-Velasquez, Joyce Lockley, Louise Lynn-Kirby and Liu Yuan at the Greater Dallas Community Relations Commission (GDCRC). Their keen insights and contributions were integral to the final version.

Jane and Dirk Velten's and Gregory Jones' skillful delivery of ACE-ing Conflict as GDCRC consultants added to its depth and usability, and their friendship has greatly deepened our understanding of the value of diversity.

Gregory's diversity values and beliefs were strongly influenced by his mentor, Dr. Charles Payne, and his multicultural education program at Ball State University. Gregory's exposure to the pedagogical genius of colleagues Dr. Gary W. Sykes, Mr. Daniel P. Carlson and Dr. Daniel T. Primozic has been another significant influence.

We acknowledge the thousands of training participants who helped us refine the suggested responses presented in this book.

Thank you to Jane Velten, who served as editor.

And we give thanks for and to our parents, spouses Tammera Buggs-Smith and David Ballard, and our children (to whom this book is dedicated) for their support and patience while we wrote this book.

Introduction

When was the last time you had a satisfying, enriching conversation about diversity? American industry has been working on valuing differences for decades now. Most, if not all, major corporations and government agencies expect their employees to value diversity. And yet, we continue to struggle with exactly how to do that. As the 2008 presidential campaigns of Senators Hillary Clinton, Barack Obama, and John McCain demonstrated, our nation still has a way to go toward the goal of respectful communications about diversity.

A number of comments made during the 2008 campaign attracted intense scrutiny. While accusations of racism and sexism have become a regular staple of the political news diet, analysts tend to examine the track record of the person who made the comment and debate whether the comment is offensive. Markedly absent from the dialogue are measured, informative and direct responses to the comments in question.

But that's nothing new. When faced with the touchy issues of race, gender, sexual orientation or religion, many usually well-spoken people have no idea what to say. As diversity trainers, we've encountered that same dilemma; only we're usually standing in front of a room of people who are expecting to hear a well-informed, dignity-preserving response to an offensive comment.

The work of a diversity trainer is challenging and difficult, *and* it's work that must be done. Drawing on our experience, we often just did our best in awkward situations, and over the years, we refined our responses based on trial and error. But it sure would have been nice to have a reference book that offered quick and accurate responses to the most commonly repeated insensitive comments and questions.

This is that book. We wrote it for diversity advocates so that you might benefit from our mistakes, and not make the same ones yourselves. However, you may make others, and if so, that is part of the process.

> **Diversity Advocates** are people who promote respect for all people and work to eliminate discrimination.

We also wrote this book to urge more people to become diversity advocates. You don't have to be a professional presenter to use the information. All of us have influence over others. And we have a number of areas of influence, including home, work, school, place of worship and community groups. Certainly if we supervise others at work–but even if we don't–we can take a stand for valuing diversity.

Finally, we wrote this book to encourage everyone to continue seeking that satisfying, enriching conversation about diversity. We believe that having such conversations–and processing our still unresolved pain and regret–will finally bring us together as a nation. We hope this book helps Americans answer Barack Obama's call to delve deeper into "the complexities of race [and other dimensions of diversity] that we've never really worked through–a part of our union that we have yet to perfect."

Each of the 50 comments in this book came from an actual incident involving a public figure, a participant in a diversity training session, or from an individual at work or in a casual setting. By recounting the comments, we do not intend to reinforce the stereotypes they offer, or to cause any distress to the groups they targeted. This is not a book of generalities, but a study of actual comments and our specific recommended responses.

Political Correctness

We recognize that not everyone agrees with the premise of this book. We know that some people strongly defend their right to say whatever they choose. And we stand firm in our right to respond.

To those who would call us "politically correct", we'll borrow a note from our own recommended response. The current usage of the term "political correctness" has done a lot of damage to the cause of diversity. It creates an image of people being forced to use sensitive and respectful language.

This book is not an instrument of force; it is a tool for those who seek one. Of course, the constitution guarantees our right to say almost anything, but most of us choose to balance that right with a desire to be respectful.

To those who say, "Sticks and stones will break my bones but words can never hurt me," we acknowledge that there are some people with extremely strong character and high self esteem for whom that adage may work.

But for most of us, comments *do* hurt. What's more, comments are usually accompanied by actions that, at the very least, exclude and often directly discriminate. This book provides tools that empower us all to advocate for the dignity and respect that everyone deserves.

To Respond or Not To Respond

Sometimes when a questionable comment is made, the setting doesn't allow for an immediate response. Sermons are just one example of this dilemma.

In these cases, we believe in saying something, even if we have to go back to the person later and reintroduce the comment. Silence, we have seen again and again, can be interpreted as agreement.

However, diversity is a topic that can provoke emotions that some people find difficult to manage. If you ever feel physically threatened or believe your safety is at risk, do not respond at all.

The Five Response Categories

For each of the 50 comments in this book, we offer five different types of possible responses: Thought-provoking, Personal, Informational, Light and Authoritative.

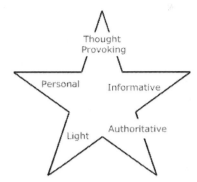

You may find one category that matches your personality closer than the others do, and so you may use that category of responses more frequently. Or you may choose the response category on a case-by-case basis, based on the other person's style or the individual setting. We encourage you to join us in trying out some of the responses that are outside our comfort zones, as we stretch and challenge ourselves to grow.

Thought-provoking – One of the most effective ways to respond to an offensive comment is to encourage the speaker to think about what has just been said. The most effective way to provoke thought is to ask a question, especially one that cannot be answered with "yes" or "no". So, we provide several questions as possible responses to each comment. In order to provoke thought rather than defensiveness, ask only one at a time and make sure your tone of voice is curious rather than accusatory. Please avoid asking one question after another in rapid fire style. Choose one of the questions, ask it, and wait for a response. Then ask another if it seems appropriate.

Personal – The Personal response allows you as an advocate to tell a bit of your own story. Admittedly, the personal responses in this book are personal to us. So if they don't represent your experience, communicate sincerely your own personal feelings and experiences. Revealing your own struggles with the issue can be very powerful because it touches the other person on an emotional level.

Informative – The Informative response provides brief factual background information when the advocate finds that the speaker is truly interested in knowing more about the issue at hand. Some of the informative responses are lengthy, so just use the portions that meet your needs. But watch out, this is where diversity advocates can get preachy!

Light – The Light response is a brief humorous, satirical, or rhetorical question or comment. Light responses are designed to avoid conflict, when you don't have the time or desire for a long conversation. They allow you to say something when you might otherwise say nothing.

Authoritative – The final response category is Authoritative. While the change they inspire may come from a different place than the other approaches, authoritative responses provide tools to employers and parents who have the ability (and responsibility, we believe) to require respectful behavior within their realms of authority. It would sound something like this, "Yes, you have a right to say that, but your job (or your television privilege) is not guaranteed to you by the constitution. You can decide to continue to engage in that behavior, and if you do, you lose the privilege."

Please note that the responses in this book are not intended to be memorized or used as a script. Instead, we encourage you to personalize them using your own style so that they feel and sound natural to you and others.

A Layered Approach

In many instances, a single response may feel incomplete. For situations in which you desire to have a longer conversation about an insensitive or awkward comment, we offer a more comprehensive process called ACE-ing Conflict.

ACE-ing Conflict requires practice, but once you become familiar with the process, you will no doubt find yourself using it often. We have used ACE successfully hundreds of times in training and in our personal lives.

ACE-ing Conflict begins with a thought provoking question, and moves on to incorporate most of the previously described response categories. ACE is readily adaptable to the circumstances at hand, and has the power to transform a charged atmosphere into a learning environment.

ACE-ing Conflict

By definition, a diversity advocate believes strongly in the value of diversity. However, passion about diversity doesn't always translate into effective communication. Often, advocates can come across to others as overbearing and "preachy".

Certainly we are within our rights to say just about anything we want in response to an offensive comment. We can choose to continue the several-year-long debate with the family member who always seems to have found a new low blow for his favorite target. Righteous anger also certainly has its place.

The point is that we do have a choice. And as we decide how to respond, an important factor to consider is whether we want to encourage change. Sometimes it's unlikely that a person is open to change.

But in those cases where we think change is possible, there is an approach that has proven effective for those who have used it.

ACE is simple and yet profound. Rather than pointing out the "error" in what has been said, this approach creates a space for people to think about what they have said.

The acronym ACE stands for Ask, Clarify, and Express. Let's examine each of the three steps, and how each step builds on the preceding one.

1. ASK a question.

When we hear an insensitive comment, our first inclination might be to come back hard with an opinion. But a much more effective response for encouraging change is to suspend our opinions for a moment, and to develop a spirit of curiosity about the speaker's perspective. Asking a question with a spirit of curiosity can be very disarming.

Why would you want to be curious when someone just said something insensitive about you (or someone you care about)? Because if you want to encourage change in that person, you need to know how she* got to the point where she thought it was acceptable to make the comment.

Why ask a question? Curious questions engage the other person by conveying interest. Questions create space for thinking. On the other hand, statements of opinions usually create defensive responses. Eventually ACE provides an opportunity for you to express how you feel, and the other person is much more likely to listen to you if you have listened to her first.

It can be very tempting to skip the question-asking step. But it is crucial. Sometimes we don't always know everything we think we know.

The best way to learn ACE is to apply it to an actual situation. Suppose someone says, "I oppose affirmative action. I think people should be hired based on their qualifications only."

---

* We utilize a system of alternating pronouns throughout the book in an effort to respect gender equity.

You may have deeply held opinions and even values regarding that subject. The natural tendency is to share them immediately. But the more change-inspiring response is to find a way to be curious about how affirmative action has affected the other person. If you make the investment of curiosity, it's likely to pay off.

So a thought-provoking question might be, "What experiences do you have with affirmative action?" Remember though, it's only thought-provoking if asked from a place of curiosity.

You will find many possible questions to ask in the Thought-provoking responses throughout the book.

2. CLARIFY the response to your question.

Clarifying is a basic communication step that many people often overlook. But it's important to clarify to make sure we accurately heard the words that were spoken. We also can clarify the emotion we believe the speaker is feeling.

Have you ever misunderstood what someone else said? Have you yourself ever been misunderstood? Most people answer 'yes' to both questions. That's why clarifying is such an important element of communication.

Clarifying also gives the other person an opportunity to think more about what is being said. Often, repeating an offensive comment in the form of a question is all that's needed. When the person who made the statement hears it back with his own ears, he may realize that what he said was insensitive. Often he'll take it back or rephrase without you ever having to say anything further.

To continue the affirmative action example, the speaker might respond to your question by saying, "I don't really have any personal experience. I just don't think it's right."

You could then clarify by saying, "So you don't think affirmative action is right. Do you feel angry when you hear about affirmative action policies?"

The speaker may or may not acknowledge anger about the issue. Either way, naming an emotion can be a very powerful clarification tool.

3. EXPRESS sincerely your feelings, beliefs and desires about the comment.

Expressing them in words means we don't have to resort to the silent treatment, slamming doors and other similar strategies.

Often the comment will not be targeted toward a group to which you belong. It is tempting but ill-advised to speak for the targeted group if you are not a member of that group. Speak for yourself and share your personal experiences, including what you have heard members of the targeted group express, if that seems appropriate.

The easiest way to make sure you're not speaking for someone else is to use "I messages". Conflict resolution is much more effective when each person speaks for himself or herself.

The following three I messages provide a simple but complete process for expressing yourself.

     a. I feel _____ when I hear that.

     b. I believe _____.

     c. I want you to _____. Will you?[1]

After "I feel", use a one-word emotion, like sad, glad, angry or proud. If you say the words "like" or "that" after "I feel", you most likely are not expressing a feeling, but a thought.

After "I believe", convey your personal value statement that informs how you see the situation.

After "I want", request the action you want the other person to take.

To continue with our example, the speaker might respond to your clarification by saying, "I guess I do feel a little angry about it."

---

[1] Therapists and mediators have used versions of this formula to differentiate feelings, beliefs and wants for decades. See *Your Perfect Right,* Robert Alberti & Michael Emmons (2008, 9th edition by Impact Publishers) for more on "I messages." The differentiation of feelings and beliefs can be traced back to Albert Ellis and Aaron Beck. Dr. Josephine Lewis, Co-Director of the Center for Cooperative Change, teaches the concept powerfully today.

You have just given the speaker the gift of tuning into his feelings. Depending on the person, that could be a very rare occurrence.

In expressing yourself, you then could say, "I **feel** both regret and appreciation for affirmative action. I do **believe** people should be hired based on their ability to do the job. I also **believe** in working to help create a society where all of us truly have an equal opportunity to succeed to the best of our abilities. And that sometimes means correcting past discrimination."

The speaker might respond by saying, "I'm not against correcting discrimination, as long as the solution doesn't discriminate again."

You could respond by saying, "Since a lot of people hire people they know and feel comfortable with, that tendency would probably increase if affirmative action went away. I really **want** people hired under affirmative action to be given the opportunity to show that they are qualified because I believe that most of them are."

You then could conclude by saying, "I'm glad you acknowledged the need for addressing discrimination. I'd **like** for you to give some thought to another solution. Will you?"

You will find many examples of expressions of feelings, beliefs and wants in the Personal responses throughout the book. The Informative and Authoritative responses in this book also are appropriate to use in the Expression step.

This exchange about affirmative action is just one example of how ACE-ing Conflict can be utilized to delve into a conversation about a sensitive diversity-related subject.

But each person who uses ACE to talk about affirmative action will apply it differently. It's a starting point that you will need to refine and personalize over time. Because the dynamic of conversation ebbs and flows, use ACE as you would a recipe that you personalize and refine over time.

Each of the 50 comments in this book can be similarly explored using ACE-ing Conflict. And we are sure that you will find many other comments and conversations to which you can apply ACE.

Teaching ACE-ing Conflict

You are welcome to use ACE in your conversations and exchanges.

For information on becoming trained in ACE-ing Conflict by a certified presenter, or to become certified to teach ACE-ing Conflict, please visit www.wordsmooth.com or send an email to info@wordsmooth.com.

Choosing Your Response

Our goal in this book is to provide layers of possible responses to offensive and insensitive comments. There will be times when you want to respond but don't choose to, or don't have time to use the entire ACE-ing Conflict process. We hope you will find in the pages that follow a rich array of choices for responding in almost any situation.

Join the conversation

In taking the journey that allowed us to develop this book, we learned as much about ourselves as we have about the rich diversity of our nation. Even though the responses we offer here have evolved over more than a decade, we have no doubt they can still be improved. We welcome your suggestions and additional comments that need responses at navigatingdiversity.com.

About Terminology

Cultural and ethnic identity is very important to most people. So at the risk of being called politically correct, we offer here the terminology guidelines we use, based on what we currently hear people calling themselves.

However, be warned: not all members of a group agree on what their group should be called. Furthermore, group names are dynamic; they continue to change. So if you use a term that someone finds offensive, respect her feelings about it, graciously accept the feedback, and use that person's preferred group term with that person.

The "Diverse" People

The term "diversity" usually brings to mind groups who are different from the mainstream. But when we use the word "diversity", we include everyone. Yet sometimes we do still need to refer to groups who historically have been called "minority groups".

The general term "minority" offends some who believe it designates an inferior position. Also, the term is not necessarily accurate; in many urban areas, people who are commonly referred to as "minority" are actually the majority. Phrases like "**people of color**" or "**communities of color**" often are used to talk about ethnic minority groups. However, you may find some who dislike those terms because it stirs thoughts of "colored people," an outdated expression that should not be used. The term "**diverse groups**" can include persons with disabilities, gay men and lesbians, seniors, and others.

Five Guidelines

Regarding what to call a specific group, we offer five general guidelines:

1. Listen to the name someone uses when describing his group to a non-member, then use that exact term.

2. If you don't know and need to use a group name, ask.

3. Specificity is usually safe. If you know a person's national origin, use it, i.e., Salvadoran.

4. When describing a condition, it is usually preferable to put the person first, as in "people with disabilities." "Disabled person" describes the person primarily by a medical diagnosis, while "person with..." describes what the person *has*, not what a person *is*.[2]

5. Never use slurs, even in an instructional manner, and even if a member of that group uses it in the course of her conversation. A number of slurs have been re-appropriated for use by members of a group but they rarely if ever are appropriate for use by someone outside the group.

---

[2] "A Few Words About People First Language," Kathie Snow, 2008, online at
http://ftp.disabilityisnatural.com/documents/PFL-Sh.pdf

Specific Group Names

African American or Black, Jamaican, Nigerian, or African, etc. Not "Afro-American", "Negro", or "colored".

Chinese, Japanese, Vietnamese, Korean, etc. **Asian** and **Asian American**, not "Oriental".

Cherokee, Apache, Lakota, etc. **Native American** is used widely across the US, but **Indian and American Indian** also are used culturally in Oklahoma and some surrounding states for legal reasons and to distinguish from **Alaskan Natives** (the preferred term in Alaska), **Hawaiians** and **Pacific Islanders**. The terms **First Nations** (used widely in Canada) and **Indigenous people** include North, Central, and South American peoples. Terms like "chief" (unless the person is actually a chief), "brave", "squaw", and "redskin" are usually considered slurs.

Gay or lesbian is usually preferred over "homosexual" or the various slurs. **Sexual orientation** or **sexual identity** as opposed to "sexual preference". **GLBT/ LGBT/ BGLT community** are three variations of a term that includes people who are Lesbian, Gay, Bisexual, and Transgender.

Indian, Pakistani, Bangladeshi, etc. **Southeast Asians.** It is not accurate to refer to this population as "Arab". The term "Asian" often is considered too broad.

Jewish people is usually preferable to "Jews".

Mexican American, Puerto Rican, Chilean, Guatemalan, etc. **Latino** (growing in popularity) **and Hispanic** are general umbrella terms which embrace Spanish speaking cultures. Only more politically active Mexican Americans use **Chicano.**

Middle Easterners refers to **Persians** as well as **Arabs.**

Muslims, not "Moslems", "Islamics", or "Islamists".

People experiencing homelessness puts the person first, as opposed to "homeless person" or "the homeless".

People living with HIV-AIDS puts the person first, as opposed to "HIV-positive" or "AIDS patient".

People with a disability, person who is disabled or **person who is differently-abled.** While **physically challenged** is accurate, it is not widely used. Not "handicapped" unless referring to the legal term.

Seniors, senior citizens, elders, older adults, rather than "old people" or "the elderly".

White, Caucasian. Non-British Whites may object to "Anglo". **European American**, although most accurate, is not commonly used.

Women, not "girls", "gals", or "ladies".

And now, here are our suggestions for handling those offensive, awkward, insensitive, questionable or uncomfortable comments. . .

1. "He's a little past his prime for this job, don't you think?"

Thought-provoking: How well do you know him? Have you interviewed him? Do you have a sense of his energy for the job? Do you think we could benefit from his experience?[*]

Personal: Someone I care about was let go from a job due to age. She was an excellent employee but didn't have computer skills. After going through a depression, she learned how to use a computer, got another job, and has been a valued employee for over 15 years. I think we vastly underestimate the value of older employees. Will you give it some more thought?

Informative: Many companies have documented the value of older employees, who tend to be knowledgeable, skilled, dependable, and loyal.[3]

Light: You'll be his age some day; hopefully, people will not judge you based on your age.

Authoritative: That's discriminatory. We don't make hiring decisions based on age. Please make your decision based on the qualifications

---

[*] Note: Remember to ask questions thoughtfully, rather than in rapid-fire fashion.

[3] *Older and Active: How Americans over 55 Are Contributing to Society* by Scott A. Bass (1995, Yale University Press)

of the candidates and what they can bring to
the position.

2. "What do you think about affirmative action? I think we should just hire based on qualification, period."

Thought-provoking: Since that's a complex issue, let's make sure what we mean by affirmative action. What does it mean to you?

<u>Follow-up questions</u>:
What qualifications do you think are most important? Is education more important that experience? Do you think if all affirmative action was stopped that employers would hire solely based on ability? So what do we do until we get there—how do we address discrimination?

Personal: I understand why you might see it that way. I have mixed feelings about affirmative action myself. I do believe people should be hired based on their ability to do the job. I also believe in working to help create a society where all of us truly have an equal opportunity to succeed to best of our abilities. But I've seen too many people hired under affirmative action have to prove themselves over and over again.

For the most part, people still have a tendency to hire those we know and those with whom we feel comfortable. I believe that tendency would probably increase if affirmative action went away. I really want people hired under affirmative action to be given the opportunity to show that they are qualified because I believe that most of them are. And I'd like for you to give some thought to another solution. Will you?

Informative: I agree. But since the EEOC receives somewhere around 80,000 charges of discrimination each year, we don't seem to be there yet.[4] Affirmative action came into being due to a lack of equal opportunity for all, as an attempt to correct past and current discrimination. And yes, affirmative action can have a negative impact in some cases. Perhaps now is the time to fully invest in alternatives, such as valuing and managing diversity.

Light: Sounds good! Now if we can just get everyone to do that.

Authoritative: Discrimination is against the law, and to ensure we don't discriminate, our company has a policy of affirmative action. You don't have to agree with it, but as long as you work here, you need to support it.

---

[4] Equal Employment Opportunity Commission "Enforcement Statistics and Litigation" online at http://eeoc.gov/stats/enforcement.html

3. **"Are you a real Indian? I've never met one before; do you live on a reservation?"**

Thought-provoking: What do you mean by "real Indian?" What do you know about American Indians? Why do you think you've never met an Indian before?

Personal: I feel sad that I myself and most other Americans really don't know very much about American Indians. I am so grateful for the survival and contributions of American Indians, historically and today. I'd like to ask you to rephrase your question. Will you?

Informative: According to the US Census, there are nearly three million Native Americans currently living in the US. When Europeans first arrived in this land, they encountered an estimated 10 to 50 million indigenous people. Over 90% of those people were killed by disease and war. Whole nations were wiped out and yet others did survive. Many were forced to live on reservations, and their descendants still do today. Many also left reservations and live in rural and urban areas all over the country.

Light: I think you might need to get out more.

Authoritative: You may not have intended it, but your question could be hurtful. I encourage you to spend some time learning about current Native American Indian culture.

4. "I'm sorry but I still feel uncomfortable if there's an Arab on my plane."

Thought-provoking: How do you know if someone is Arab? Do you fly often? What experiences with Arabs on airplanes have you had that influenced your views? What would it take for you to feel comfortable flying with someone who is Arab on the plane?

Personal: September 11, 2001 saddened and angered me. I am trying very hard to keep my anger directed toward those responsible, and not extend blame to others who look like them or come from the same part of the world as they did. I find that many times, my emotions are influenced by my thinking. I want you to give this some more thought. Will you?

Informative: The vast majority of Arabs and Muslims condemn terrorism.[5] Effective airport security experts recognize that if they focus only on people who they think may be of Arab heritage, they can easily miss someone intent on doing harm to others. Terrorists can capitalize on the shortsightedness of racial profiling by utilizing someone who doesn't fit the profile. When security efforts focus on

---

[5] "Muslim-Arab world condemns Islamic terrorism after London attacks", Edward M. Gomez, *San Francisco Chronicle*, 7-12-2005 online at http://www.sfgate.com/cgi-bin/article.cgi?file=/gate/archive/2005/07/12/worldviews.DTL ; also "Muslims Condemn Terrorists" online at http://www.muhajabah.com/otherscondemn.php

suspicious behaviors like buying a ticket with cash or not checking any baggage, they achieve better results in identifying potential terrorists than when the focus is on ethnic background.[6]

Light: Maybe you should think about renting a car.

Authoritative: While I understand your safety concern, it is unfair to a large number of people who are just trying to get somewhere like you are. Racial profiling is not the solution.

---

[6] "Profiling," Security expert Richard Schneier, August 15, 2005, online at http://www.schneier.com/crypto-gram-0508.html

5. "Tran told me he's from Houston. But does anyone know where he's really from, originally?"

Thought-provoking: What would it take for you to believe he's originally from Houston? Where do you think he might be from? What makes you think he's not from Houston?

Personal: When I meet someone who doesn't look like a European American, I'm automatically curious about the person's country of origin or ancestry because I love geography. I don't always ask about it, though, unless I have a chance to first establish some rapport. I also remind myself that many people who don't have European ancestry are born and raised in the US.

Informative: Historically, the media has consistently portrayed Asians as foreigners. We can be influenced by those images without really realizing it. But over a third of Asians and Pacific Islanders now living in the US were born here.[7]

Light: Do you want to know the name of the hospital where he was born?

---

[7] Facts for Features, Asian/Pacific American Heritage Month May 2005, US Census online at http://www.census.gov/Press-Release/www/releases/archives/facts_for_features_special_ed itions/004522.html

Authoritative: If he told you he's originally from Houston, then believe it. If you want to know where his parents are from, then ask him after you've gotten to know him better.

6. "Blacks are really good at sports and music."

Thought-provoking: Are all Blacks good at sports and music? Do you know any Blacks who don't excel at sports or music? What other skills do African Americans have? What skills are involved in excelling at sports and music?

Personal: I love spirituals, jazz, blues, reggae, zydeco—all Black styles of music that evolved in the Americas. I have loved watching Venus and Serena Williams, Michael Jordan and Tiger Woods. I also regret that, historically, most African Americans had only a few career paths like these where they could really excel. I feel sad that, as a whole, most Americans don't know very much about those who broke through barriers and made important contributions in science, medicine, business, literature, and other fields. I'd love to explore the topic in more depth with you. Are you game?

Informative: Many Blacks are good at sports and music, but it is inaccurate to say that all are. Entertainment and sports are two fields where talent eclipsed discrimination relatively early. In many other fields, however, discrimination still eclipses talent. In any field, when discrimination barriers fall, members of groups that have been denied opportunities are then able to develop their talents and excel.

Light: Those are two areas where discriminatory barriers fell early.

Authoritative: That is a stereotype that holds a kernel of truth but is also very limiting. Please think more carefully about what you are trying to say.

7. **"In the end, Blacks will prevail over Whites because what goes around comes around."**

Thought-provoking: What goes around comes around? What would that look like to you? Would that be justice?

Personal: I think slavery and segregation were reprehensible and tragic; both for what the practices did to those taken from Africa and for what they did to those who stayed in Africa. I do hope and believe that people of African ancestry all over the world will continue to prevail over the obstacles in their way. Even when it seems justifiable, I feel sad when anyone takes revenge on someone else. I don't believe it repairs the harm, and I do not believe it is just.

Informative: Anger and the desire for revenge are normal human reactions to severe oppression like what Africans suffered under slavery and segregation. If the anger and pain are not processed and healed, they will continue to simmer and from time to time, boil over. When South African Apartheid fell in the 1990's, the government established a Truth and Reconciliation Commission to give people a way to process their pain. As a nation, America has had no similar way to process our historical pain. However, when discrimination barriers fall in any field, members of groups that have been denied opportunities are then able to develop their talents and excel. Excelling at these opportunities is another outlet to channel the anger constructively.

Light: Hopefully we are learning to live together.

Authoritative: I certainly hope that we all do our best to excel. But I want to see Blacks and Whites working on teams together, not operating out of a racially competitive mindset.

8. "That boy's finger does not need to be on the [nuclear weapon] button."[8]

Thought-provoking: How old is the person you're talking about? Did you know that term is offensive to most Black men?

Personal: Sometimes I can't believe the things that come out of my mouth. That's because I'm influenced by a culture that developed when racism was out in the open. I strongly regret that anyone ever tried to make a grown man feel inferior by referring to him as a "boy".

Informative: The word "boy" is considered extremely offensive by most African-Americans because, during the Jim Crow days, many southern White people often referred to grown Black men as "boys" to assert their supposed racial superiority.

Light: At what age does a boy become a man in your neck of the woods?

Authoritative: The person you refer to is a man. Please don't refer to grown men, especially Black men, as boys. It's offensive.

---

[8] "GOP lawmaker apologizes for Obama remark", MSNBC, 4-15-2008, online at http://www.msnbc.msn.com/id/24122867/

9. "Why does that guy always have a chip on his shoulder? He thinks everyone owes him because he's a minority."

Thought-provoking: Why do you think he acts the way he does? Have you ever asked him about his experiences? How would you like to see him behave?

Personal: I've been known to be in a bad mood now and then, sometimes over something that may seem minor to others. If he's in a bad mood a lot, maybe he's been through some hard times.

Informative: It doesn't take very many experiences of discrimination for a person to become wary and self-protective, especially if the discrimination happens early in life. One or two negative experiences as a child can lead a person to make life decisions that may not serve him well as an adult. But he may not know how to make a change. It's possible that he has internalized the negative information that he received and on some level may not believe he is a valuable person. If that is the case, he is sure to act out those beliefs out in ways that drive people away from him.

Light: Well, at least we do owe a lot to his ancestors, if you think about it.

Authoritative: I don't think it serves the environment here to have negative comments made about people who are not present. I encourage you to bring the matter directly to him with a professional and solution-oriented attitude.

10. "I'm color-blind. I don't see color when it comes to people."

Thought-provoking: What leads you to say that? Are you sure that people don't want you to see their color? Is there something negative about seeing color? Is it the noticing that's problematic, or is it the judgment that often follows?

Personal: I don't want you to ignore my color. I think it has a lot to do with who I am. I believe it's important not to judge, but I actually enjoy noticing and appreciating differences.

Informative: Some people think that Martin Luther King, Jr. was urging us to be color-blind when he said he hoped that one day his children will be judged not by the color of their skin, but by the content of their character. But he used the word 'judged." He wasn't urging us not to notice differences. He was urging us not to judge based on our differences. When a person of color is asked if she wants her color to be ignored, the answer is usually 'no.' Skin color is often tied to cultural heritage and important experiences that are meaningful and worthy of attention.

Light: If you closed your eyes, I bet you could tell me the color of my skin.

Authoritative: Trying to be color-blind is really not the best way to value diversity. There's nothing wrong with noticing differences. Let's recognize and celebrate our differences.

11. "I fear for my parents. They have lived in the same place for 30 years. The neighborhood has changed since they moved there. It is mostly Black now, and there is a lot of crime. I worry about them."

Thought-provoking: What problems have they had? Do you think it is the ethnicity of the neighborhood that has led to the increased crime rate? Could it be the economics of the area that leads to crime?

Personal: I think it's natural to worry about your parents. I know I do. But I want to make sure and focus my concern on the actual threats. I try to remind myself that crime is the concern, and not so much the color of the people living nearby.

Informative: Unfortunately, some people believe race and crime are linked together. But the vast majority of research on crime shows a connection between poverty and crime. Usually, economic conditions that lead to social ills tend to drive high crime rates. Some suggest the best fix for crime is education and equal access to legitimate means of support or equal opportunity. There are several theories that address crime causation, including strain theory, conflict theory, broken window theory, and more.[9]

---

[9] *The Color of Justice*, Samuel Walker, et al. (2004, Thomson – Wadsworth)

Light: I think we're talking economics rather than ethnicity.

Authoritative: Safety should be a concern in all neighborhoods, regardless of ethnicity. So get in contact with a crime prevention specialist with the local police department. They will come out and inspect their home in order to make sure that they are as safe as possible, and they will also give your parents tips on keeping safe when they are out and about.

12. "Why does every group have their own chamber of commerce? If there was a White chamber of commerce everyone would be up in arms."

Thought provoking: Why do you think there are so many chambers of commerce? When do you think the Black and Hispanic chambers of commerce were developed? What was going on at that time in those communities? Thinking about the history of discrimination, is there anything to be said for communities taking initiative to improve their situation? Do you think a White chamber of commerce would improve our community in any way?

Personal: I hear this concern a lot. I have been involved in the various chambers of commerce and I think they are all important. I believe there is still a role for ethnic chambers because I believe that businesses headed by people of color still face obstacles. I want to ask you to think a little deeper about the history of discrimination before making this comparison again. Will you?

Informative: Today's individual chambers were developed at a time when their members were not served by the existing chamber of commerce. Most minority-owned businesses continue to have different needs and focuses than larger, majority-owned businesses. Each individual chamber is able to focus on the specific needs of its members and community, and in the process, add value to the overall community.

Light: For a long time the chamber of commerce was the White chamber of commerce without the name.

Authoritative: You may not be issuing a subtle call to form a White chamber, but some could interpret it that way. That would be reversing the progress that has been made. When all discrimination has been eliminated, then we might see a decreasing need for various chambers. However, we are not even close to that point yet.

13. "Why don't Blacks and Hispanics do as well as Whites in school? Don't they understand the value of education?"

Thought-provoking: What do you think? What measurement of disparity are you using–test scores, graduation rates, degrees earned? Why do you think there are still disparities? Do you think Hispanics and African Americans would say that they don't value education? Thinking about the Hispanic and Black experiences in America, what barriers might there be to education for these groups?

Personal: I think there are a number of factors at play, not the least of which is racism. I certainly do not believe it has anything to do with the innate intelligence of any group. I have observed in my interaction with all groups of people that they value education. Sometimes that education is formal and other times it is informal, but learning tends to be an important value for all the groups with whom I interact. Even if formal education seems unreachable, it is still valued.

Informative: The education gap between Blacks, Hispanics and Whites continues to confound the education community. Numerous studies conducted to assess the problem contradict each other. Causes probably include a combination of income disparities, inherent bias in the preparation of test instruments, school overcrowding, less experienced teachers teaching in lower income areas, historical segregation, continuing institutional racism such as low teacher expectations, and more. But education is one of the topics in almost every conference and public discussion in the African American and Latino communities. Often these barriers also cause resentment that can be interpreted as a lack of appreciation for education.

Light: What might look like not valuing education may actually be the priority of survival and providing for the family.

Authoritative: I applaud your interest in this difficult challenge facing our country. I encourage you to carefully research some of the current information out there to become more informed. And I want to encourage you to reconsider how you stated your opinion. It came across as a stereotype.

14. "That elite silver-spooner has no idea what it's like on my side of the world."

Thought-provoking: How do you know? What do you mean by "silver-spooner?" What is it like on your side of the world? How much do you know about his side of the world?

Personal: It's sad to me that we have a label for just about everyone. Even when we are trying to remove barriers and increase understanding, we find labels standing in our way. I believe labels separate us, no matter what they are. I want to ask you to look past the label and get to know him as a person. Will you?

Informative: Privilege certainly can offer protection from the dangers and problems that face people of limited income. Philosophers like Karl Marx and others believed that private property is one of the biggest separators of people. Yet quite a few people from privilege come upon hard times, or even take steps intentionally to learn first hand what life is like without their privilege.[10] You never know for sure about someone's personal experiences until you get to know him.

Light: I wonder if he's as judgmental as you just were.

Authoritative: Name-calling and labeling are

---

[10] For example, John Howard Griffin, author of *Black Like Me* (1961, Houghton Mifflin).

not acceptable here. Get to know him before you decide what you think about him.

15. "Go back where you came from."

Thought-provoking: Where do you want her to go? What do you know about where she is from? What do you know about why she is here? Are you intentionally trying to be hurtful?

Personal: I get angry when I hear that comment. It feels so discounting of the person and her history. I believe that one of our country's greatest strengths is its diversity, which was accomplished mostly by immigration. I want all visitors and citizens to be treated respectfully while in America.

Informative: Since all White Americans are the descendants of immigrants or are immigrants themselves, telling a person of color to go back where they came from is one of the most ironic insults around. Most European Americans had more choice in their immigration to the US than did most people of color. Most Africans didn't choose to come to America. American Indians and Mexicans were already here. And many Asian immigrants in the 18th and 19th centuries were brought to America to work for extremely low wages building railroads and doing other menial work.[11] Many of the more recent Asian immigrants from South Vietnam, Laos and Cambodia were escaping war.

---

[11] "Chinese American Contribution to the Transcontinental Railroad", Central Pacific Railroad Photographic History Museum online at http://cprr.org/Museum/Chinese.html

Light: How boring of you to repeat that tired insult.

Authoritative: If you have a disagreement with someone from another culture, you have lots of options for expressing it without resorting to that insult. I don't know what gave you the impression that we tolerate that kind of comment here, but let me assure you if you say something like that again, you likely will be looking for another job.

16. "God d@#! America for treating our citizens as less than human."

Thought-provoking: Are you saying that you believe God should condemn or has condemned America? In what ways has America treated citizens less than human? Are you aware of how deeply that comment cuts many Americans?

Personal: I feel a strong reaction to what you said. I agree with you that there have been and continue to be injustices against many Americans. But I believe that using that language pulls us further apart.

Informative: No doubt about it, our nation's history is replete with injustices like slavery, Jim Crow, segregation, racial profiling and the near genocide of Native peoples. At the same time it has offered unprecedented freedoms and opportunities for success. The difficulty seems to be finding a way to discuss our shortcomings while recognizing our strengths.

Light: I really don't think anyone knows who God will condemn.

Authoritative: Statements like that, while they may have a kernel of truth, can be very alienating. Since we are working to ensure that everyone feels valued, please rephrase your statement.

17. "Support for Black candidates among working, hard-working Americans– White Americans–is weak."

Thought-provoking: Why do you think that might be? What could White Americans do to increase their comfort level with Black candidates? When you say "hard-working Americans–White Americans," are you communicating a link between those two groups? Will you tell me more about how you see hard working Americans?

Personal: I really try hard to base my decision on a candidate's positions. But sometimes I notice unconscious prejudices in my own decision-making. I know I often stumble in trying to talk about racially sensitive issues. When I do, I always make an intentional effort to clarify and apologize for muddying the issue.

Informative: White working class people consider many factors in deciding who to support. But race still seems to play a role for a significant minority of White working people in some places. 2008 primary exit polling revealed that race was a factor for 16% of West Virginians and 18% of Kentuckians, two states that are over 95% White and have large working class populations.[12] These numbers really are

---

[12] "Did racism win West Virginia, Kentucky for Clinton?" by About.com online at http://racerelations.about.com/b/2008/05/21/did-racism-win-west-virginia-kentucky-for-clinton.htm

not surprising when we consider the history of racial politics in the region.

Light: That's not too surprising to hard-working Black Americans.

Authoritative: I'm sure you didn't intend to link the words "hard-working" only to White people, but some could have heard it that way. Please be more careful as you discuss these historically difficult topics.

18. Do you really believe in the Holocaust?

Thought provoking: Why do you ask? What about the Holocaust is important to you? Are you aware of some theories that dispute the Holocaust? How are those positions supported?

Personal: I have talked with/read accounts written by people who were held in Nazi concentration camps. I believe that these people are telling the truth about the horrors they witnessed and endured. I get angry when I hear someone minimize this tragedy.

Informative: There is nearly unanimous consensus by mainstream scholars on the Holocaust that the evidence given by eyewitnesses, survivors,[13] photographs,[14] and even the documentation by the German government itself proves that over six million Jews and other ethnic minorities, prisoners, people with disabilities and mental illness, gay men and political activists were killed by the Nazis during World War II.

Light: If I could wish it away I would, but it did indeed happen.

Authoritative: It's not really a matter of belief. The Holocaust of World War II is well

---

[13] Voice/Vision Holocaust Survivor Oral History Archive online at http://holocaust.umd.umich.edu/

[14] *Auschwitz: A History in Photographs* by Jonathan Webber, (1993, Indiana University Press)

documented. If you have a different perspective, I encourage you to carefully consider how well researched it is.

19. "The Bible says the gay lifestyle is wrong. And God used Hurricane Katrina and AIDS as punishments."

Thought-provoking: Have you had the opportunity to get to know a gay man or lesbian? Do you think your opinion might be different if you did know someone personally? What do you think about the non-gay people who have died of AIDS and were hurt by Katrina? Do you believe people choose to be gay?

Personal: I feel uncomfortable with making that kind of judgment. I'm sure I've done things the Bible says are wrong but I don't believe it's my place to judge a person's sexuality. I don't believe that illnesses or disasters are punishment for sin. Babies get AIDS and I don't believe they did anything to deserve it.

Informative: Punishable actions usually involve a choice. There have been many studies conducted to determine whether sexual orientation is biological or environmental. There is no consensus. Homosexuality has occurred in all human cultures throughout history and also has been documented in several animal species. Many experts say that sexual orientation develops early in life and there is little to no evidence that sexual orientation can be changed. Most gay men and lesbians report that they do not experience their sexuality as a choice.[15]

Light: That's not the God I know.

Authoritative: Religious beliefs and sexuality are personal matters. I don't want to see anyone condemned for either. I doubt very much if all of the 1800+ people who died in Katrina were gay.

---

[15] "Gay brothers may hold genetic clues", 10-15-2007, MSNBC News online at http://www.msnbc.msn.com/id/21309724/; "Homosexuality" Wikipedia entry online at http://en.wikipedia.org/wiki/Homosexuality

20. "Why do we have all these hyphenated Americans? Why can't we all just be Americans?"

Thought-provoking: Why do you think some people combine their ethnic heritage with their national identity? Does it mean they are not fully American if they do so? Why might it be more important to some groups than to others?

Personal: I feel a sense of loss that my family/many families did not retain more of our ancestral identities. I have looked into my genealogy and researched some of the cultures in my background. It's become important to me to know where I came from, and I am always glad when I see a family that still teaches its history to the new generation.

Informative: A Mexican American is simply an American whose heritage is from Mexico, and who feels the cultural connection strongly enough to reference it as part of his identity. Most European Americans have found it to their benefit to drop any reference to their European heritage. An African American traces her ancestral heritage back to the continent of Africa; usually for American Blacks, this means West Africa. The term "African American" originated from within the group itself, which accounts for its popularity.

Light: We *are* all Americans. The more we work to make sure everyone feels like a fully valued American, the less we'll have to focus on what we call ourselves.

Authoritative: All of us have a right to self-select what we want to be called, and groups usually choose names that have a significant historical and cultural meaning to them.

21. "It won't be long before the illegal aliens change the name of our country to the United States of Mexico."

Thought provoking: What are your experiences with immigrants? How has immigration affected you? Where did you hear those terms?

Personal: I believe illegal immigration is a complex issue that requires a serious cooperative effort to address. So I get sad when rhetoric gets in the way of honest dialogue. I have met many undocumented immigrants, and I have never run into anyone with that plan in mind. The Mexican immigrants I know simply want to make a living, become Americans and maintain their cultural heritage. I believe the term "alien" is designed to alienate. So I don't use it.

Informative: Illegal immigration has recently become a controversial political debate in which economics, politics, culture, anti-terrorism and anti-foreign sentiment all have played a role. While a leading Harvard immigration economist showed a positive impact on the US economy of $10 billion from immigration, he believes immigration should be limited because he found that it depresses wages of lower-skilled native workers.[16] While

---

[16] "Migration Washes Over Ambivalent America," by Alvin Powell, *The Harvard University Gazette*, February 2000, online at

preventing terrorism and maintaining cultural continuity are valid concerns, they also can be used as veils for anti-foreign sentiment. I believe that if we stay focused on our highest common values, we will be able to create a workable solution that addresses all of the valid concerns.

Regarding the country's name changing, the British immigrants who were in the majority when this country was named did not choose to name it the United States of Britain. Did you know that "America" is the feminine version of the Italian name Amerigo, for Amerigo Vespucci, an explorer who discovered that the "new world" was separated from Asia?

While the term "illegal alien" is legally valid, it connotes not just foreignness, but strangeness and other-worldliness. "Illegal immigrant" and "undocumented immigrant" are other accurate terms that can help keep the focus on solutions.

Light: Nah, I think we'll keep our Italian name.

Authoritative: I think that is a little over the top. There are more constructive ways to communicate your concerns about immigration.

---

http://www.hno.harvard.edu/gazette/2000/02.24/i_George_B orjas.html

22. Someone tells an insensitive joke.

Thought-provoking: Was that a joke? Do you get many laughs when you tell that joke? Where did you hear that joke? What do you think (a member of the targeted group you both know) would say about that?

Personal: I just don't feel comfortable with jokes like that. Stereotypes aren't funny to me. I want you to stop telling that joke. Will you?

Informative: Jokes like that may seem harmless, but that's what makes them quite dangerous. Because they seem harmless, they get passed along by and to people who wouldn't intentionally discriminate. Jokes subtly influence our thinking even though we don't realize it. That's how stereotypes survive and thrive, unintentionally passed along through jokes.

Light: I don't get it.

Authoritative: There is plenty of humor out there without resorting to insensitive jokes. Please find a different joke to tell.

23. "[That woman should just] iron my shirt."

Thought provoking: Oh, is your shirt wrinkled? Do you need to borrow an iron? Was that intended as a joke? Who did you imagine would find that funny?

Personal: I feel angry when anyone's potential is restricted by stereotypes and limited thinking. I have personally benefited from the leadership of women and I hope to soon see the day when women's contributions are fully appreciated.

Informative: Throughout history, many patriarchal societies have viewed women as subservient. In some instances, women were considered property rather than people. Yet many societies have long recognized the value of feminine leadership, and countries on every continent have had women leaders.[17]

Even though the Civil Rights Act of 1964 made discrimination based on sex illegal, the vast majority of top American leadership positions are still held by men.

---

[17] "Women Prime Ministers and Presidents: 20th Century", Jone Johnson Lewis, About.com, online at http://womenshistory.about.com/od/rulers20th/a/women_heads.htm

Light: Iron your own shirt.[18]

Authoritative: If you have a concern about someone's qualifications, you have plenty of options for expressing it without resorting to insults. I don't know what gave you the impression that we tolerate that kind of comment here, but if you say something like that again, you could be looking for another job.

---

[18] This response is courtesy of a woman in the crowd at the event where this insult was repeatedly hurled at 2008 presidential candidate Hillary Clinton.

24. "I really jewed-down the price."

Thought-provoking: What do you mean by that? Where does that term come from? Where did you hear that term? How do you think Jewish people feel about that term?

Personal: I feel uncomfortable with that term because a friend of mine who is Jewish told me it's hurtful to most Jewish people. I want to ask you to stop using it. Will you?

Informative: The stereotype that Jewish people are skilled at handling money originated with the Christian and Muslim prohibition against usury, or lending money with interest. The Jewish tradition allowed the practice, and so Jewish people were able to develop the trade.[19] Of course, not all Jewish people have wealth or are skilled at finances. And today, money lending with interest is widely accepted in Christian nations.

Light: That's one I haven't heard in a while.

Authoritative: That term comes from a stereotype about Jewish people. I'm sure you don't mean to stereotype anyone, so please don't use that term.

---

[19] "Usury" Wikipedia entry online at http://en.wikipedia.org/wiki/Usury

25. "This is one nation under God, but the liberal atheists want God totally out of this country."

Thought-provoking: What does the concept of one nation under God mean to you? Are you connecting liberalism to atheism? Have you ever met a liberal religious person?

Personal: I really like the balance of the First Amendment, especially the section that says that the government shouldn't be involved in the establishment of religion, nor should it prohibit the practice of religion. I believe everyone has the right to choose whether and how they relate to a higher power. As we work toward truly being "one nation", if someone tries to impose specific religious beliefs onto another, I think we get further away from that goal.

Informative: The words "under God" were added to the pledge of allegiance in the 1950s. America's principal founders, George Washington, Thomas Jefferson, John Adams and Benjamin Franklin, had quite liberal views of religion and were very suspicious of government involvement in religion.[20] After four or five weeks of contentious deliberation during the Constitutional Convention of 1878, Benjamin Franklin, who doubted the divinity of Jesus,

[20] Rick Shenkman, "An Interview with Jon Butler ... Was America Founded as a Christian Nation? " December 20, 2004 on the History News Network website online at http://hnn.us/articles/9144.html.

made a motion to bring in a minister for a prayer. He was voted down.[21] Thomas Jefferson, who rejected the divinity of Jesus, but nevertheless considered himself a follower of Jesus, rewrote the New Testament without the parts he believed were inauthentic.[22] The founders of America were religious liberals who established the principle of the separation of church and state.

Light: The phrase "nation under God" was never used by the framers of the constitution.

Authoritative: Religious beliefs are personal matters. I don't want to see anyone judged for their beliefs or non-beliefs.

---

[21] Catherine Drinker Bowen. *Miracle at Phaladelphia: The Story of the Constitutional Convention, May to September 1787.* New York: Book-of-the-Month Club, 1966, pp. 125-126, as cited by the Quartz Hill School of Theology at
http://www.theology.edu/journal/volume2/ushistor.htm.
[22] *The Life and Morals of Jesus of Nazareth Extracted Textually from the Gospels in Greek, Latin, French and English* (published in 1820) is more commonly known as the *Jefferson Bible*.

26. **"Why do we need to learn about all these other groups? They should learn about us [Whites]. This is a democracy. Doesn't majority rule?"**

Thought provoking: Do you feel more comfortable not knowing about the history of other groups? Can you think of an example of when it might be valuable to know about diverse groups in America?

Personal: I personally love learning about the richness of American culture and all the unique and fascinating individuals in our history. I also feel very sad when I think about the children who don't have the knowledge of their culture's contributions to America. I believe this lack of knowledge deeply affects their self-esteem.

Informative: The framers of our Constitution created a republic—a representative form of government—for that very reason, so the rights of a minority are not tread upon by the will of the majority. Learning about other groups helps us all gain more appreciation for each other. If we appreciate each other, we're more likely to defend each other's rights.

Light: People of color know more about Whites than you realize. They have to, to survive.

Authoritative: If our goal is to promote harmony and create a society where all are valued, then yes, we need to learn about each American culture.

27. "Why can't we just go back to the melting pot? My ancestors gave up their heritage to become American. Why can't everybody?"

Thought-provoking: Where did your ancestors come from? Did they choose to come to America? What things did they give up— language? Food? Customs? Music? Their names? Why do you think your ancestors gave up their heritage or culture? Was it a choice? What do you think their response would have been if they had been punished for observing their cultural traditions, speaking their language, etc? Do you think we ever achieved the melting pot? Who melted? Were there groups who didn't melt? Why do you think they didn't?

Personal: I personally feel a sense of loss that some of my ancestors gave up a lot of their heritage. I don't think it was worth it in the long run. Rather than a melting pot, I prefer the image of the salad bowl because it suggests a creative and tasty mixture of different ingredients. While each ingredient retains its own flavor, each also complements another and combinations create new flavors.

Informative: The way most Americans live today is based largely on the culture of England—language, laws, music—but certainly with huge influences from the other cultures that are represented in the US. Many European immigrants did choose to give up some aspects of their heritage, while many others clung to theirs. That's why there are places like Little

Italy and Germantown. The idea of a "melting pot" never really worked completely, but it worked well enough for Europeans, for whom it was intended. However, the melting pot was never intended to include Blacks, Indians, Mexicans, and Asians.

Light: I wonder how truly willingly they gave it up.

Authoritative: Don't expect everyone to do what your ancestors did. The melting pot was about making everyone the same. I encourage you to move forward toward valuing diversity and appreciating differences.

28. "The problem I have with Islam is that Muslim women have to be subservient to their husbands."

Thought-provoking: Are you sure about that? Do you think all Muslim women are subservient? Do you think that subservience is a condition of the religion, or is it a cultural expectation in some parts of the world? Do some members of other religions expect to be subservient?

Personal: I feel sad when I hear generalities like that. To be categorized as subservient hurts and discredits all the strong Muslim women I know. I would love to see men of all religions work to reduce sexism.

Informative: My understanding of Islam is that both men and women are called to submit to God. There are cultures and religious groups all over the world–including some Christian groups–that interpret their religion to limit the development of women. But Islam declares men and women equal before God.[23]

Light: My female Muslim doctor would tell you otherwise.

Authoritative: That statement is inaccurate. I encourage you to study Islam and to question stereotypes like that before repeating them.

---

[23] Frontline's "Women and Muslims" at http://www.pbs.org/wgbh/pages/frontline/shows/muslims/themes/women.html

29. "We don't have any problems here."

Thought-provoking: Wow, no problems here? Does anyone have a different opinion? What kinds of assessments have you done to determine that? If someone felt uncomfortable, do you think you would hear about it? Okay, is there any room for growth here?

Personal: I believe that all humans are imperfect, and therefore, in any relationship, there are problems now and then. Usually in my relationships, when I don't think there's any problem, it means that I just haven't been paying attention. I have worked with a lot of organizations and all have at least a few issues that need improvement.

Informative: Sometimes problems or concerns can lie beneath the surface. Even if there are no obvious issues at the moment, if a space was made for people to bring their concerns, we might hear things we never expected to hear. You know better than I do if you are actually taking inventory.

Light: I'm glad to hear that. So this is a great opportunity to review how you're managing diversity.

Authoritative: I would nevertheless like to encourage open mindedness as we discuss the issue. If the shoe fits, wear it. Just use what you believe applies to you. But don't reject it outright.

30. "This just sounds like a lot of political correctness to me."

Thought-provoking: What does that mean to you? What would it mean to you if someone called you politically correct?

Personal: I'm sorry you think so. I think the term "political correctness" has done a lot of damage to the cause of diversity. It brings up an image of people being forced to use sensitive and respectful language. Of course, the constitution guarantees our right to say just about anything, but I hope most of us want to balance that right with the desire to be respectful.

Informative: Valuing diversity is about finding a sincere respect for all groups so that society and its organizations can benefit from everyone feeling valued. It really has nothing to do with correctness; it's about effectiveness.

Light: If being respectful is politically correct, then I'm okay with that.

Authoritative: There is always a choice. You have a right to your beliefs. However, your actions need to reflect the principle of respect for all.

31. "I'm prejudiced against Oreo cookies."

Thought-provoking: Are you referring to the actual cookie or using the derogatory term?

Follow up questions:
Have you tasted an Oreo? Is there a recipe that insures that all Oreos are exactly the same? What about people? Are any two people exactly alike?

Personal: I could engage in a conversation about cookies and prejudice, but I really want to talk about human prejudice against other humans. That's the important and uncomfortable work that I know I need to do, and want to ask you to join me in doing. And I do feel uncomfortable with the way some people use the term "Oreo" to put down Black people.

Informative: I'm not sure if you are aware, but "Oreo" is a derogatory term used to describe people who are said to be Black on the outside and White on the inside. This description in itself is limiting because it assigns certain characteristics to Whites and Blacks that are not truly restricted to one group or the other.

Regarding prejudice against the cookie, since all Oreos taste exactly the same, you wouldn't have to try every Oreo in order to know that you don't like them. You have enough information to decide. But no two people are exactly the same. That is where the analogy breaks down. When we are prejudiced against a whole group of people, without having met each one, we are not using valid information in making our decisions.

Light: Well, just as long as you're not prejudiced against *people*. That's really my concern.

Authoritative: Please be careful how you use the term "Oreo" because it can be used as a put down to Black people. Talking about food preferences really gets away from our focus, which is prejudice against different groups of people. I know it may be uncomfortable, but let's tackle this issue.

32. "I am not prejudiced, but I don't believe in race mixing and I think all this diversity stuff just promotes race mixing."

Thought-provoking: How would you define prejudice? What concerns you most about race mixing? What about my comments leads you to think I'm promoting race mixing?

Personal: I'm not sure how you came to that conclusion. I deeply believe that all people are equally valuable and deserve equal respect. If they choose to be in relationship with each other, that is their right. But it is not my mission to make that happen.

Informative: Race mixing is a confusing term because there really is no anthropological basis for the different races we were taught about in school. The most recent scientific conclusion about race is that there is just one–the human race, and all members of the human race have always been able to produce children with each other. Diversity advocates promote respect for all people and work to eliminate discrimination. Very few, if any, promote cross-cultural relationships as a priority goal.

Light: Won't it be great when everyone realizes we're all members of the human race?

Authoritative: I assure you that my goal is not to promote race mixing. The idea is to learn about each other; about our similarities and differences. Our goal is to free our society of discrimination, and I encourage you to support that goal.

33. "She's a religious fundamentalist; she doesn't do complicated."

Thought-provoking: What do you mean? Do you really think her religion tells you very much about her mental capabilities?

Personal: I don't want to be judged based on my religious identification. So I try hard not to judge anyone else on that basis either.

Informative: Religious fundamentalists are employed in all fields at all levels of responsibility. Fundamentalists are deeply committed to the infallibility of the Bible, which they believe outlines important moral principles and values. While some non-fundamentalists might see that commitment as simplistic, the struggle between faith and modern societal elements is quite complex. And since not all fundamentalists are literalists, they must understand the complexities of scriptures in order to know how to apply them to daily life.

Light: That's a pretty uncomplicated analysis of her capabilities.

Authoritative: That is a stereotype that is very limiting. When you give a person the opportunity to prove her capabilities, you don't have to resort to stereotypes.

34. "That's so retarded."

Thought-provoking: What do you mean? What does the word "retarded" mean to you? Are you talking about an intellectual disability?

Personal: Someone close to me has an intellectual disability and he is a wonderful and lovely person. I don't really like the word "retarded" when it's misused in that way. So I want you to stop using it. Will you?

Informative: Many words and phrases that we use without even thinking can be extremely hurtful. People with developmental and intellectual disabilities historically have been called "mentally retarded", but the word "retarded" is also used frequently these days as a put-down. So, children and adults with these conditions have to deal with their actual challenges, as well as social judgments.

Light: Will you use a different word, please?

Authoritative: Please don't use that expression. It's hurtful to people with intellectual disabilities.

35. "Why do we always have to keep hearing about slavery? That was over 200 years ago, already."

Thought-provoking: Why do you think it is still brought up? Is there anything left to say about slavery? Why is it uncomfortable to talk about slavery? Is it possible that some of the issues we are facing today have a link to slavery?

Personal: I feel sad and angry when I read or see a film about slavery. It is incomprehensible to me that slavery existed at all. I think when each generation of young people grasps the gravity of slavery, they experience a need to express and process the emotions that go along with understanding how awful it really was. I know I felt that need, and I still do sometimes. I also believe that many of us *think* we've had the conversation when we really have just skirted around the edges of it.

Informative: If we want to move forward and make progress, history is certainly an important teacher. Philosopher George Santayana said those who don't learn from their history are doomed to repeat it. It's important to recognize that fairness did not instantly materialize when President Lincoln emancipated enslaved people in 1863. African Americans were released from bondage with no means to make a living, so they often stayed right where they were. Those who tried to improve their lot were often punished with beatings and death. Between 1882 and 1964, groups like the Ku Klux Klan committed over 4,700 lynchings in order to maintain White supremacy.[24] The Supreme Court ruled segregation legal in 1896. It was only in the last 50 years that things began to move toward fairness and yet, fairness is still not achieved. The more we know about slavery and what followed it, the more we begin to understand the issues we continue to face today.

Light: I'm not sure you've had the real conversation about slavery.

Authoritative: While you may believe that you have heard enough about the subject, I would encourage you to be open to everyone's opinion on slavery. Bottom line: no one in this organization has the right to deem this conversation off limits.

---

[24] "The Negro Holocaust: Lynching and Race Riots in the United States, 1880-1950", Robert A. Gibson online at http://www.yale.edu/ynhti/curriculum/units/1979/2/79.02.04 .x.html

36. Someone uses a slur.

Thought-provoking: What was that? Who have you heard using that word? What led you to decide to say it? What do you think (member of the targeted group you both know) would say about that?

Personal: I feel uncomfortable with that word, and I'm asking you to please stop using it.

Informative: That word is generally considered offensive. While the constitution protects free speech, the use of that term alienates a lot of people—those within the targeted group—as well as others who value diversity. If the goal is to maintain separation from that group, that's one way to do it. But most workplaces and community organizations will not accept the use of that word.

Light: Did you just say the [letter]-word?

Authoritative: That word is offensive and I don't ever want to hear you say that again.

37. "I can say (slur) to my close friend. We joke around like that all the time."

Thought provoking: Have you ever asked your friend how she truly feels when you use that word? Are you sure you would get an honest answer? Have you ever laughed at something while inside you felt uncomfortable?

Personal: I feel so uncomfortable to hear you say that. I would feel very awkward using the term with anyone, even more so with a friend. I've seen how deeply people have been wounded by slurs and I've made a commitment to myself never to use them at all. I want you to really stop and think about it. Will you?

Informative: You may never really know what your friend thinks about you using that word. Many groups have words they use with each other that they object to hearing from someone outside the group. Often a group reclaims or re-appropriates an offensive term to use internally in order to reduce the negative impact. But it is one thing for a member of a group to use the word. It is another thing entirely for someone outside the group to use it, because there's always a possibility that it's coming from a different motivation. And even though he may not say it, it's quite possible your friend feels uncomfortable.

Light: I wonder if you're as close as you think you are. (or) There's got to be another way to show how close you are.

Authoritative: I think you should be really careful with using slurs in any setting. It is not okay to use slurs here, period.

38. "I don't think people should speak Spanish in mixed groups. I don't understand what they're saying. Maybe they're talking about me."

Thought-provoking: Is it your concern that you're being talked about that leads you to say you don't want Spanish to be spoken in mixed groups? How many languages do you speak fluently? Have you ever tried to learn a second language? What do you think they might be saying about you?

Personal: I love languages and wish I knew more than one fluently. I respect those who can speak more than one language. Rather than ask them to speak only English, I value the opportunities I have to hear people speak languages other than English so that I can try to learn a little bit. I don't believe it's fair to ask people not to speak in their native tongues just to make me more comfortable. Will you take some time to rethink your position?

Informative: People usually feel most natural communicating in their first language. There is also a cultural connection that happens through language. If one person greets another in their common language, it would be disrespectful not to respond in the common language. In mixed groups, there is usually someone who will gladly translate if asked.

Light: More than likely, they're not talking about you.

Authoritative: The ability to speak more than one language is valuable. Rather than trying to limit cultural expression, we should be trying to expand our language abilities. Talk to the people who are having conversations in Spanish and ask them to include you.

39. "Why do some Black people talk White but most Blacks speak slang?"

Thought-provoking: What do you mean by "talk White?" Are you talking about standard English vs. Ebonics? Do you know any White people who use slang?

Personal: I wish I had a linguistic link to my ethnic roots. (or) I'm glad I have a linguistic link to my ethnic roots. I'm sad that so much negativity surrounds Ebonics. I wish that Americans could have the same respect for African Americans' cultural way of speaking as we do for Cajun language and culture, for example.

Informative: Great question, because conflict is often rooted in miscommunication. Standard English is a way of speaking English that was defined by Whites, and of course English itself came from English people, who historically were White. Today, however, anyone can speak standard English. There are many variations of English spoken in the US, such as Cajun, Southern, New York City and Boston English.

Ebonics or Black English is believed to be an adaptation of English to the language patterns of many West African languages. Linguistic scholars studying Ebonics have demonstrated similarities in sentence structure, tonality and vocabulary to many West African languages.[25]

---

[25] *African American English: A linguistic introduction*, Lisa Greene (2002, Cambridge University Press)

So its roots in African American history distinguish it from simply *wrong or bad* English. That Ebonics has survived over so many generations all over America is a result, at least in part, of segregation. Today, some African Americans look upon Ebonics with cultural pride, others pride themselves on speaking standard English, and many are bilingual. Many books and dictionaries are dedicated to preserving Ebonics.

Light: You know, your question had about as much slang as it did standard English.

Authoritative: Anyone can speak standard English while still retaining a cultural identity other than English. No one should be judged or shamed based on speaking style. Whether a person speaks in the style of his cultural roots or a more standard style of English, or both, is no reflection on his skills and capabilities.

40. "She's trailer trash. She can't help it that she doesn't know how to dress."

Thought-provoking: Where did you hear that term? How do you think she would feel if she knew you said that?

Personal: I feel very uncomfortable when I hear that term. Someone who is very close to me comes from a low income background and I know how much she has been hurt by comments like that. Will you stop using that term?

Informative: Mobile homes provide housing at a lower cost than a conventionally built house. So people with limited incomes do often live in mobile homes. However, people with limited incomes are no less valuable than are people with higher incomes. Trash signifies something that is thrown away. No human being should be thrown away. And fashion sense transcends income level. Plenty of people with high incomes lack fashion sense.

Light: I bet she has better manners than you just exhibited.

Authoritative: That's a hurtful term. Don't use that to describe anyone, please.

41. "I'm tired of people asking for handouts. Welfare is weakening our society."

Thought-provoking: How does welfare affect you personally? Do you know anyone who has been on welfare or another government assistance program? How does welfare weaken society? How would you like to see our society help people in need if not with welfare?

Personal: I'm sad to hear you say that, because I (or someone close to me) was a beneficiary of welfare. Being able to have some assistance when we needed it saved my family from the most desperate of situations. I think keeping people from desperate situations strengthens rather than weakens a society.

Informative: Welfare has been the focus of a lot of discussion and reform. While most of us probably think of adults when we consider welfare, children are the major beneficiaries of welfare. Welfare reform has had mixed results, depending on who is doing the reporting. Most former welfare recipients found work, but a significant number did not. While income levels seem to have gone up overall, most former recipients remain poor due to low wages.[26] On the other hand, many people who received

---

[26] "Welfare Reform 10 Years Later" The Joyce Foundation, 9-01-2006 online at
http://www.joycefdn.org/Publications/PublicationDetails.aspx?pubId=9

assistance have gone on to be productive members of society.

Light: Helping people in need is a worldwide value.

Authoritative: You are entitled to your opinion, but your statement is overly broad and judgmental. We are all in this boat together.

42. "White males are the ones without any rights. We are the only ones not protected by the government from getting fired."

Thought-provoking: In what way have you felt your rights unprotected? Will you tell me more about that?

Personal: I'm sorry you feel unprotected. That is a very uncomfortable feeling. I want to assure you that you are protected against discrimination.

Informative: Sometimes it can seem that the emphasis on diversity leaves out White men, which has caused some White men to reject diversity efforts. But the goal of valuing and managing diversity is to create an environment where we all are respected, have rights and are appreciated for who we are. And who we are includes our differences.

I assure you, White males are covered under anti-discrimination laws and are protected from being discriminated against based on race, gender, age, disability, veteran status, etc. Any target of discrimination is protected under the law. A case of discrimination against a White male is just that—a case of discrimination. It's not reverse discrimination, as it is often called. Discrimination against White males is not the most often reported type of discrimination, but it does happen.

Light: They're doing pretty well to lead over 90% of American companies without any rights.

Authoritative: While you might not intend it, your statement is provocative. Whites certainly are protected under the same laws as everyone else. I encourage you to bring us your concerns and experiences without making reckless statements like that.

43. "I don't think it's true that I'm treated better because I am White. That just doesn't sit right with me."

Thought provoking: You don't believe that you are treated better because of the color of your skin? What would it mean for you if it were true?[27]

Personal: I don't like it either. And yet, the more willing I am to see it, the more obvious it becomes to me. I want you to watch how people interact more objectively and think about it some more. Will you?

Informative: Often it is easy to miss if you have never been made aware of it. A few years back, Diane Sawyer did an informative special called "True Colors" featuring a Black guy and a White guy who had the exact same background. She documented the preferential treatment salespeople, landlords, and cab drivers gave to the White guy. But even he didn't realize he was getting better treatment. It took the cameras to prove the disparity. Dr. Peggy McIntosh of Wellesley College has done some interesting work documenting what she calls "the invisible knapsack of White privilege."

Light: Try trading places with an African American.

---

[27] This beautiful question was asked by Lee Mun Wah in his film "The Color of Fear", available at StirFrySeminars.com.

Authoritative: While it is very difficult for most White people to acknowledge White privilege, I encourage you to sit with the idea for awhile; don't reject it outright.

44. "There's a reason that we've never had a woman president. Women are too emotional to do that job."

Thought-provoking: Is an effective president one with little or no emotion? What women have you known that you thought were too emotional? Why does it seem that emotion is incompatible with leadership? Are there other reasons we haven't had a woman president?

Personal: I think emotion is what makes us human. I would be very afraid of a president who didn't feel emotion or who didn't understand his or her emotions, since all of us have them.

Informative: There is a growing body of research on the importance of emotional intelligence. Psychologist and author Daniel Goleman has shown that people who are not comfortable with and don't understand their emotions do not make the most effective leaders.[28] And yet many Western societies discourage men and women—and most especially men—from learning this skill. What's really problematic then is that men often make decisions based on emotion without even knowing it because they have learned to deny and hide their emotions.

---

[28] *Emotional Intelligence* by Daniel Goleman (1995, Bantam Books)

Light: Emotions are integral to being human...We could use more of that in the Oval Office.

Authoritative: That kind of judgment has no place here. We know from experience that women are capable leaders.

45. "I disagree with you 110%."

Thought-provoking: Okay, what's your take on the issue? Tell me how you see it.

Personal: I'm disappointed to hear that, because I feel strongly about what I'm saying. But that's the nature of this work—we won't all see it the same way.

Informative: Disagreement is actually a starting point because it allows discussion. And sometimes we find after discussion that we don't disagree as much as we first thought.

Light: Wow, that's a lot of disagreement.

Authoritative: Okay, for time's sake maybe we should agree to disagree and move on.

46. "Would you let your child date someone of another race?

Thought-provoking: How is the issue of diversity, children and dating important to you? Is it uncomfortable for you to imagine your child dating someone of another background?

Personal: I've known people of different backgrounds who have wonderful relationships, and others who have a difficult time getting along. My restrictions have more to do with the attitudes and behaviors of my children's friends. But if all people are equally valuable, then I can't see how it makes sense to place an arbitrary restriction like skin color on whom my child can date.

Informative: Today's youth are growing up with more messages of equality between ethnic groups than ever before. So it's no surprise that this generation feels less inhibition about cross-cultural dating. Yet what has been called inter-racial marriage still occurs at a very low rate. Laws prohibiting interracial marriage existed until 1967, when a married couple, arrested for living together, appealed their conviction all the way to the Supreme Court. These laws were then finally declared unconstitutional, but it took some states much longer to comply. In 2000, Alabama became the last state to remove language prohibiting interracial marriage from its constitution.[29]

Light: My child is only allowed to date members of the human race.

Authoritative: Child rearing is a topic that deserves a lot of attention and discussion. But romantic parameters in the end come down to a parent's personal decision. I don't want my opinion on this topic to detour us from our focus on ensuring that every person is valued and appreciated.

---

[29] "Anti-miscegenation laws" by Wikipedia online at http://en.wikipedia.org/wiki/Anti-miscegenation_laws

47. "You're a liberal."

Thought-provoking: What does the term liberal mean to you? Is your willingness to hear what I'm saying affected by how you see liberals?

Personal: I don't object to that term. But I believe that labels can get in the way here. I just want a society where all people are respected and treated with dignity.

Informative: Valuing and managing diversity is not a liberal or conservative issue. All sides of the political spectrum have come to understand the importance of valuing and managing diversity.

Light: Let's set aside the labels for now.

Authoritative: I don't think we can afford to see diversity as a liberal issue. Diversity is important and must be respected by all—liberals and conservatives and everyone in between.

48. "You are bashing White men."

Thought-provoking: Help me understand, what did I say that came across as bashing White men? How can people discuss this issue without coming across as bashing White men?

Personal: I'm sorry if that's how it came across because that is not my intent. That's really the last thing I want to do, because White men are so important to the success of diversity initiatives.

Informative: The conversation about discrimination is challenging because it requires that we examine our history. There's no way around the fact that White men were at the helm when this country's discriminatory policies were put into place. Understandably, it is uncomfortable for most White men to hear that said if it seems that they are included in the indictment. But you are not to blame for the societal ills of discrimination. The goal in valuing diversity is to have these discussions without anyone feeling that he personally is being blamed.

Light: Please try not to take historical events personally.

Authoritative: I do not mean to bash White men. Nor am I going to beat around the bush when it comes to American history. Eighteenth century White men did set up the American system and its institutions to benefit themselves, and their great-great grandsons still benefit from it today. While there's no sense in blaming 21st century White men for our history, it is important that they take some responsibility to make positive changes now.

49. "You're getting defensive."

Thought-provoking: How does that affect your willingness to hear me and consider what I'm saying?

Personal: That could be. These issues are very dear to my heart, and some of the things you said may have pushed my buttons. Let's both try harder to listen to each other, okay?

Informative: I must admit, I am *passionate* about this subject and sometimes my passion can be mistaken for *defensiveness*. Our cultural communication patterns may also be bumping into each other.

Light: Thanks for pointing that out!

Authoritative: Duly noted. Nevertheless, I need you to hear what I'm saying and take it to heart.

50. "You're stereotyping."

Thought-provoking: Help me, what did I say that you believe is a stereotype? What did I over-generalize? How might I have said it differently without stereotyping?

Personal: I thank you for bringing that up. I may have already mentioned that, although I do consider myself a diversity advocate, I still have to work at it. I do have room to grow and I appreciate it when someone gives me an opportunity.

Informative: Let's review the definition of a stereotype: "A generalization without enough information." So it is possible to make some generalizations about groups if we have reliable information, and those generalizations would not be considered stereotypes.[30] If most members of a particular group generally agree that their group has a certain tendency, then we are more likely talking about a cultural practice than a stereotype.

Light: Just checking to see if you were listening!

Authoritative: The example I gave is based on measured observations of group behavior. A stereotype is based on a lack of information. While there are sure to be exceptions, this tendency does appear to be a cultural practice

---

[30] For instance, most Latinos acknowledge that their culture is family-oriented, even though there are exceptions.

of this group, as cited in (cite source). In order to understand and appreciate our diversity, sometimes we must speak to those group differences.

Diversity Training Traps

51. "You tell me your prejudices and I'll tell you mine."

Thought-provoking: How do you think that would be beneficial? What's your goal in suggesting that exercise?

Personal: I've seen many people get hurt during those types of conversations. I don't want to engage in something that's counterproductive. I want us to stay on track and tackle today's agenda. Will you stay with us?

Informative: The focus of today's agenda is [explain objectives]. The subject nature of prejudice is so emotional that it is really crucial to have not only a significant understanding of the issues but also a deep level of trust between participants. If you seriously want to pursue this idea, I'll recommend a planning session to build an advanced session into the program.

Light: Nice try, but I'm not going there with you.

Authoritative: No. No matter how objective we might try to be, someone is going to be insulted and/or hurt. It's a lose-lose exercise.

52. "My boss should be here in this class."

Thought-provoking: What are we discussing that you think will benefit your boss? How would that improve your work situation? What can you do to bring the information back to your boss? Even if your boss isn't here, how can those who are here benefit?

Personal: Sometimes, I find myself listening to a sermon or message and thinking about whom else needs to hear it. If I'm honest, I often find that those thoughts are a way to deflect attention from what I need to learn myself. I want to ask you to focus more on how the content applies to <u>you</u>. Will you?

Informative: Everyone, truly, can benefit from this class, and I hope your boss will be in a session soon. It is very difficult to make changes in an organization unless its leadership is invested. And, at the same time, the course is designed to give you tools you can use with anyone, whether he or she is committed to valuing diversity or not.

Light: Your influence on your boss may be greater than you think.

Authoritative: Yes, I agree. But since you are the one here now, I hope you gain what you can from the session.

53. "This class isn't going to change anything. It's just window dressing."

Thought-provoking: What in your experience tells you that things will not change here? What kinds of changes do you think need to take place? What do you think we need to do differently in order to give you hope for real change? What does anyone else think?

Personal: I'm frustrated to hear you say that. I have absolutely no desire to be window dressing. I am personally and deeply committed to what we are presenting and believe that your organization can benefit greatly from it.

Informative: If all the organization does is training, you are correct; change will be minimal. True organizational change requires goal-setting and the implementation of a strategy that includes accountability measures. What people are held accountable for, they usually begin to prioritize. Then training becomes seen as relevant and people seek it out.

Light: We really hope it opens the door or at least a window to some new ideas.

Authoritative: You may be frustrated with past diversity efforts, and still I encourage you to bring an open mind to this session. Allow each person to get as much out of it as she can.

54. A training participant accuses another of being racist, and is citing a specific incident in which they were both involved.

Thought-provoking: Do you believe this is the best place to have this important conversation? Could this be discussed during a break or after the session?

Personal: I've had a similar situation occur personally, and it was much more effective to discuss it in private, one-on-one.

Informative: This is the kind of disagreement that does come up in a diverse workforce from time to time. It just reinforces the point that we don't all see things the same way. The challenge is for each of us to really try to see the other person's point of view. And that is best done in a private setting.

Light: Let's take a break so you can deal with this privately.

Authoritative: I'm going to ask that we take a break now, and I am available to work with you through this issue.

55. Training participants opt out of the session or engage in horse play.[31]

Thought-provoking: What's going on at that table there, anyone? What made you decide to (name the action)? Does this content create some discomfort for you?

Personal: When we're not all focused, I can get distracted. So I want to ask you to be patient and rejoin us. I value your perspective, so if you don't agree, please let me know. I can't really utilize what you're doing right now.

Informative: Often kidding around can signal discomfort with the topic of diversity. That's why we developed an interactive session with the adult learner in mind. We know there are all types of learners, so we have videos, activities, and discussions. If a certain part of the course loses your interest, please stick with it, because it won't be long before we switch gears again.

Light: It seems we've touched a nerve.

Authoritative: Your behavior is disrupting the session. Would you like to rejoin the rest of us or are you opting out of training? If you decide to opt out, I am obligated to inform your employer which session you missed and my assessment of your comprehension of the topic.

---

[31] Physically standing near the participants who are opting out while you respond may increase your effectiveness.

56. During a training session your co-trainer gets into a rather extended exchange with a training participant.[32]

Thought-provoking: As we process that exchange, what is at the core of your reaction? How is this exchange indicative of the challenges we still face?

Personal: You know, I have a strong reaction to that as well. How about anyone else?

Informative: This exchange demonstrates how emotional the issues of diversity can be. Certain comments and topics can trigger past experiences that may yet be unresolved. Until they are healed, there is always a risk that they will provoke strong reactions.

Light: We may need to agree to disagree on this one.

Authoritative: I can see that _____(the participant) and my partner are very passionate about this issue, but it doesn't look like we are going to resolve it right now. So why don't we take a short break?

---

[32] Physically standing between the two parties while you respond may increase your effectiveness.

Moving Forward

(Don't Skip This Part!)

You've made it through 50 comments and our suggested responses. Now what?

Keep in mind that this book is *written* communication. *How* you say what you say is just as important as *what* you say. When we say *how*, we mean your tone of voice, intonation, and the words you emphasize. Communication experts call the *how* portion of what you say the para-verbal.

According to many experts, when we talk, only seven percent of the meaning we communicate is in the actual words. A much larger 38 percent is para-verbal, and 55 percent is completely non-verbal (i.e., body language and facial expressions).

Take, for example, the word "great." If you say the word "great" with a happy tone in your voice and you smile, you will convey the traditional meaning of "very good." But if you say the exact same word using an angry tone while throwing up your hands, you will convey the opposite meaning.

So, the template of responses we have provided gets you seven percent of the way toward the communication you want to convey. We strongly suggest that you go over the comments that concern you most and practice the responses that feel most comfortable to you. We also encourage you to step out of your comfort zone and try some that don't feel completely comfortable. And pay attention not only to the words, but *how* you communicate these suggested responses. If your *how* is off, many of these suggested responses can come off as snappy comebacks or gotcha's.

If your response is received as a gotcha, the result is not likely to be desirable, and in some extreme cases, you may even be putting your safety at risk. So please pay special attention to this issue. We are not qualified to mend broken noses.

In order to hone your *how*, we invite you to rediscover the lost art form of curious listening. In order to effectively respond, you must be sure what was said. That requires listening, which is the core principle of the ACE Approach outlined on pages 6-12 in this book. If you want to encourage dialogue, a curious demeanor intent on tuning in to the other person is the key. To "actively" listen, clear your mind and focus on what is being said in an effort to understand. Be careful to avoid the tendency to listen with the goal of one-upping, or simply waiting for a pause so you can get in your opinion.

The **speaking/processing gap** is a good reason to actively listen. Most humans can speak at a rate of 125 words per minute or so. However, experts say our brains can process upwards of 400 words per minute.[33] That leaves a several hundred word gap. That gap is why you often may be able to complete someone else's sentence. But sometimes that completion isn't accurate. If we do not fully listen, we can go off on tangents, offer useless advice, or

---

[33] For instance, "Personal Coaching – Active Listening," James Manktelow, Mind Tools, July 2004, online at http://www.mindtools.com/pages/Newsletters/29July04.htm

tell a story of our own that has little relevance, all because we didn't fully listen to hear and understand what was actually being said. So when someone is speaking, remember to slow down your mind and tune in.

> "Grant that I may not so much seek... to be understood as to understand."
>
> - St. Francis of Assisi

Being an advocate of diversity isn't easy. But when you listen curiously and seek to understand, you'll recognize that some people make insensitive comments simply to get a reaction. Other people make comments out of simple ignorance. In such cases, beginning with a thought-provoking question and utilizing the ACE-ing Conflict process may be more appropriate than starting with any of the other suggested responses.

People who make insensitive comments out of ignorance usually are trying, but they simply may not know how to express themselves in a culturally sensitive manner. So, handle them with care. If your response causes them to feel uncomfortable or embarrassed, you may have lost an opportunity to make a friend and build up an ally.

In the end, the most important bit of advice we can give you is this: when reacting to questionable comments, model the respect you want to see.

Good luck with your work. We invite you to let us know how it goes—both your successes and bloopers—at NavigatingDiversity.com. We also provide a resource page there with links to organizations that can support your work.

About the Authors

Patty Bates-Ballard is a mother, freelance writer and editor who advocates respect for the earth and its people. Owner of WordSmooth, a communications company, Patty works from her Dallas home where she and her husband, David, raise their two sons, Kory and Kaden.

She has written numerous articles on the topics of diversity, ecology, wellness and politics. Her "Socha" diversity + effectiveness workshop series helps school districts, corporations and non-profit agencies "Sow, Cultivate, and Harvest" their organizations' full potential.

Patty's extensive experience as a conflict resolution specialist, diversity trainer and mediator with the Greater Dallas Community Relations Commission (GDCRC) helped her develop an honest and effective communication style that engages the listener. Patty's faith, combined with her involvement in civil rights efforts, has given her a deep appreciation and respect for cultural and ethnic differences that inform all of her endeavors. She earned degrees in Psychology and Philosophy from Austin College.

The anti-racism efforts of the Unitarian Universalist Association's Journey Toward Wholeness program, the fabulous JTW team at First Unitarian Church Dallas, Visions, Inc. and Crossroads Ministries have informed Patty's understanding of institutional racism. She balances those challenging perspectives with the mediation training she received from Dallas' Dispute Mediation Center and the dialogue coaching of Nancy C. Wonders.

The National Coalition Building Institute's Prejudice Reduction and Controversial Issues models have also been influential as she works with people of disparate viewpoints to find common ground.

Gregory Smith has facilitated diversity education programs for over 20 years. Currently, Gregory serves as a training director for The Institute for Law Enforcement Administration (ILEA), a division of The Center for American and International Law, where he develops and administers law enforcement training programs in the areas of police management and supervision, ethics and ethical decision-making and diversity education.

Gregory teaches police personnel throughout the United States and Canada. Qualified to administer the Meyers-Briggs Type Indicator, he also lectures on Ethical Leadership, Developing Effective Teams, Conflict Resolution and Coaching through Psychological Type.

He earned a Bachelors of Science from Ball State University in Sociology with a Minor in Multi-Cultural Education, and has completed 39 hours of graduate work at Baylor University and the Universities of Texas at Dallas and Arlington. Gregory also served in the United States Army and the United States Army Reserve for 21 years and progressed in ranks from private to major.

Gregory's diversity values and beliefs were strongly influenced by his studies at Ball State University. As a student in the Multi-Cultural Education program, Gregory's mentor, Dr. Charles R. Payne, academically prepared him to communicate with and teach people from mountain regions of the U.S. to federal reservations, and from inner cities to the rural south.

Gregory's vision of a nation where we can respect each other's differences, and even honor them, has been strongly influenced by colleagues Mr. Gregory Jones, *Baylor University Medical Center*, Ms. Diane Berg, *University of North Texas*, and Mr. David Snoddy, *Ontario Police College, Aylmer, Ontario Canada*.

Patty and Gregory met in 1995 when they were both relatively new to the field of diversity training. Both strong Intuitive Thinkers on the Myers-Briggs Type Indicator, they have collaborated together on numerous training projects over the years. Gregory participated in and facilitated many of the GDCRC's programs and Patty has been a periodic presenter for ILEA in Gregory's Diversity Train the Trainer program.

Their professional friendship has been of great importance to them both. It has weathered many questionable comments as they have bravely explored diversity-related topics that many colleagues try to avoid, including politics, race, gender, religion, homosexuality, and more.

Made in the USA
San Bernardino, CA
13 September 2017